W9-ATV-622

SKILLS Coach

America's Best for Student Success

Write It Out

Mastering Short and Extended Responses to Open-Ended Questions

LEVEL D

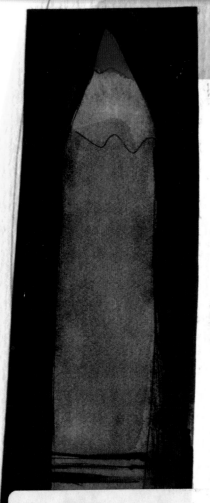

Sheila Crowell & Ellen Kolba

SKILLS Coach™
America's Best for Student Success™

Write It Out

Mastering Short and Extended Responses to Open-Ended Questions

LEVEL D

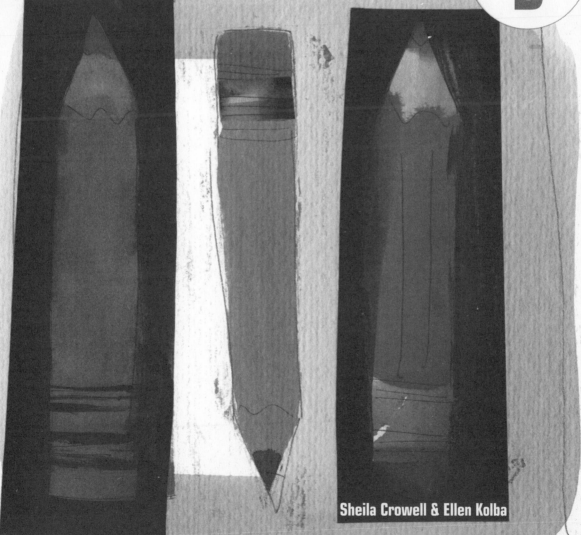

Sheila Crowell & Ellen Kolba

About the Authors

Sheila Crowell and **Ellen Kolba** are specialists in the teaching of writing and in preparing students for writing assessments. Their textbooks provide the affirmative support and scaffolding all students need to become better, more confident writers and to improve their scores on writing assessments.

As staff developers and writing curriculum specialists, Crowell and Kolba show teachers how to evaluate writing by first identifying and specifying the strengths in a draft, then making suggestions based on those strengths to prompt revision. To support the teaching of writing in their own school district in Montclair, New Jersey, they developed **The Writers' Room**™ program, which trains volunteers from the community, pre-service teachers, and students to serve as writing coaches in elementary, middle, and high school language arts and English classes.

Under their direction, **The Writers' Room**™ program has been brought to schools in Elizabeth, Metuchen, and Trenton, New Jersey, as well as to districts in New York, California, and Canada.

Acknowledgments

Special thanks to our writing team for their help with this book:

Caleb E. Crowell

Marsha Kalman

Write It Out, Mastering Short and Extended Responses to Open-Ended Questions: Level D
126NA
ISBN# 1-59823-027-1

EVP, Publisher: Bill Scroggie
VP, Editorial Director: Marie Spano
VP, Creative Director: Spencer Brinker
VP of Production: Dina Goren
Art Director: Farzana Razak

Senior Development Editor: Elizabeth Jaffe
Contributing Editor: Lisa Trumbauer
Authors: Sheila Crowell and Ellen Kolba
Designer: Sydney Wright and Kathrin Ayer
Layout Artist: Kathrin Ayer
Cover Design: Farzana Razak
Cover Photo: Julie Delton/Photodisc/Green/Getty Images

Triumph Learning® 136 Madison Avenue, New York, NY 10016-6711
© 2006 Triumph Learning, LLC

A Haights Cross Communications, Inc. company

Printed in the United States of America.

10 9 8 7 6 5 4 3 2 1

Table of Contents

Part A: Writing Short Answers

Table of Contents

Part B: Writing Extended Answers

Table of Contents

6

In school, you have to take lots of tests.

Many test questions give you a choice of answers. You must pick the correct answer from the list of choices. Questions like these are called **multiple-choice questions**.

Another type of test question asks you to write something in your own words. Questions like these, which ask you to write your own answers instead of choosing from a multiple-choice list, are often called **open-ended** questions. They might also be called **constructed-response** or **extended-response** questions. This book is about these kinds of questions.

Open-ended questions are important! An open-ended question counts for more on a test than a multiple-choice question does. So it's important to learn how to write good answers to this kind of question.

Your score on an open-ended question depends on two things:

1) How well you understood the reading selection.

2) How well you expressed your answer in writing.

This book will give you practice doing both.

An open-ended question may call for a short answer or an extended answer.

🌀 A short answer contains only a few sentences or a paragraph.

🌀 An extended answer may take two paragraphs or more—even a page.

In this book, you will practice writing both short and extended responses to open-ended questions. By the time you get to the end of the book, you should be ready to handle most open-ended questions on a real test.

So let's get started!

5 Rules for Writing Good Answers

Open-ended questions are based on a reading selection. When taking a test that asks open-ended questions, you first need to read the selection. Then you answer the questions that follow. In order to practice writing answers to open-ended questions, you need to start with a reading selection.

When you turn the page, you'll see a selection for you to read. Read it carefully. All the questions in the rest of this introduction are about this selection. You may read the selection as many times as you like if you need help to answer the questions.

As you read the questions and answers, you will also discover five good rules for writing good answers. We call these rules the *SLAMS* rules. At the end of the introduction, you'll see why.

Now turn the page to begin reading about the gobbling grasshoppers.

8

Read the selection and answer the questions that follow.

Gobbling Grasshoppers

Grasshoppers!

They were everywhere. One woman wrote that her farm was so thick with grasshoppers that the ground seemed to be moving.

The grasshoppers ate the grass. They ate the leaves on the trees. They ate the farmers' crops. They ate tool handles and gnawed at fence posts. Families threw blankets over their gardens to try to save the plants, but it didn't work. The grasshoppers ate the blankets. Then they gobbled up the gardens. For dessert, they ate the family's laundry.

These were not ordinary grasshoppers. Grasshoppers usually live by themselves. They do not form large groups. In the 1870s in the American Midwest, thousands of grasshoppers were born at the same time. They traveled in swarms to look for food. They were a kind of grasshopper called the Rocky Mountain locust.

No one knows how many grasshoppers swarmed over the plains states during the 1870s. Each winter, they would die, but the following summer they appeared as black clouds, falling from the sky like snow. Some people said the grasshoppers numbered in the billions. Others guessed trillions. One swarm was more than a hundred miles wide and almost two thousand miles long! They ate their way from Canada to Texas.

Many farm families had nothing left. They chose to leave their farms, while others tried to stick it out. They nearly starved.

In 1876, the swarms became smaller. The last Rocky Mountain locust died in 1902. Nobody has seen a Rocky Mountain locust for more than a hundred years. They are extinct, gone from the earth for good.

But no one knows why.

Here is an open-ended question you might find on a test:

> **The selection tells about gobbling grasshoppers. What did the grasshoppers do?**

Hector's Answer:

> ### ate things

Hector's answer is correct. The grasshoppers did eat things. But Hector's answer probably would not get a good score. Why? It is not written in a complete sentence.

Hector's answer would have been better if he had written it like this:

> ### The grasshoppers ate up all the farmers' crops.

> ## Rule 1
>
> Answers to open-ended questions should always be written in complete sentences. (Exception: When you fill out a chart.)

> **What other things did the grasshoppers eat besides crops?**

Here is another open-ended question:

Hector's Answer:

> ### lots of things

Rewrite Hector's answer so that it would get a better score.

Write your answer here.

_____

_____

_____

10 — Rule 2: <u>L</u>ine Length=Answer Length

When writing the answer to an open-ended question, it's sometimes hard to know how long your answer should be. Here's a rule to help you know:

If your handwriting is big, you'll take about one and a half lines to write a sentence. If you write small, you'll need only one line for a sentence.

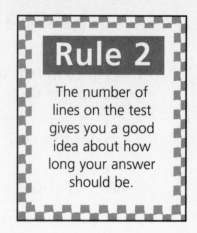

Rule 2

The number of lines on the test gives you a good idea about how long your answer should be.

✓ So, if you see three or four lines, you probably should write at least three sentences.

✓ If you see a whole page of lines, you probably should write at least two paragraphs.

✓ If you see two whole pages of lines, then you should write at least three paragraphs, maybe more.

Nidia read this question on a test:

> **How many grasshoppers made up a big swarm?**

Nidia's Answer:

<u>Nobody knows how many grasshoppers made up</u>
<u>a big swarm.</u>

_____

_____

_____

Can you figure out what Nidia did wrong? Nidia is correct, but her answer is too short. It does not have enough details from the selection.

On the lines after Nidia's answer, add more details about how many grasshoppers made up a big swarm. Remember to write in complete sentences.

This is harder than it looks! You have to be careful. You must answer all parts of the question, and you must give information that belongs with the answer. For example, look at this question:

> The selection says that grasshoppers are usually solitary. What does that mean?

Victor's Answer:

The selection says that grasshoppers are usually solitary. Sometimes they come together in big swarms and eat everything they can.

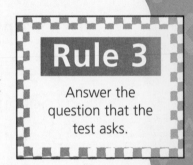

Rule 3

Answer the question that the test asks.

Denise's Answer:

The selection says that grasshoppers are usually solitary. That means they live by themselves. They don't usually form groups with other grasshoppers.

The facts in both answers are true, but Victor's answer is not a good one. **He did not answer what the question asks.**

✓ The question doesn't ask what grasshoppers do when they are not solitary. It asks what the word <u>solitary</u> means.

Denise's answer is much better. She answers the question that was asked.

Try it. Answer this question, using the information in the selection:

> What did the farmers do when the grasshoppers ate their crops?

_____

_____

_____

Rule 4: <u>M</u>echanics Count

12

When writers—or teachers—talk about "mechanics," they don't mean people who fix things. In writing, mechanics means spelling, punctuation, and capitalization. Mechanics also means grammar and good word choices.

Suppose you write a good answer, but it has a few mistakes in spelling or punctuation. You will not get a low score. But suppose you make a lot of sloppy or careless mistakes. Then you will lose points.

Read the question, and then read Josh's answer.

> **What did an attack of horrible grasshoppers look like?**

Josh's Answer:

frist it looked like a blak clowd then it looked like the cloud was snowing grasshopers soon there was so many grasshopers that it looked like the grownd was mooving.

Rule 4

Mechanics are important! Your sentences should have no mistakes.

What do you notice? Josh's answer has a lot of supporting details, but it would not get a high score because Josh did not pay attention to mechanics. His answer has:

✓ 6 spelling mistakes. All these words are spelled wrong: *frist, blak, clowd, grasshopers, grownd, mooving*

✓ A long run-on sentence. The answer should have been written in three sentences.

✓ 3 mistakes in capitalization. The first word in each of the three sentences should begin with a capital letter.

✓ 2 missing periods (at the ends of the first two sentences).

✓ A mistake in grammar. The second *was* should be *were*.

Rewrite Josh's answer with no mistakes. (HINT: All the misspelled words are spelled correctly in the selection.)

_____

_____

_____

This is probably the most important rule of all. Many students don't pay enough attention to it. If you forget everything else, remember this rule!

Support means to include information that explains or adds to your answer. This is very important! Some or all of the support for your answers must come from the selection. For some questions, it's OK to add your own opinions, but you MUST include some information from the selection in whatever you write!

Rule 5

Support your answers with details from the selection.

For example, read two students' answers to the following question:

> **What happened to the grasshoppers after the great swarms of the 1870s?**

Lee's Answer:

The grasshoppers disappeared. It seems strange to me. How can a trillion insects all disappear? I'll bet they are still around somewhere. I'll bet they'll be back someday.

Sue's Answer:

There were a few small swarms. Then the grasshoppers stopped coming. Nobody knows why, but they are all gone. The last one died in 1902. Nobody has seen one for over 100 years.

Read the question again. Then read Lee's and Sue's answers. What do you think about their answers?

Answer the questions below to show your ideas.

Did Lee do a good job of telling what happened
to the grasshoppers?   ___Yes ___ No

Did Sue do a good job of explaining what happened
to the grasshoppers?   ___Yes ___ No

Below are details that Lee and Sue wrote in their answers. Check which details are from the selection and which are NOT from the selection.

Lee:
The grasshoppers disappeared.

___**from the selection**   ___**NOT from the selection**

It seems strange to me.

___**from the selection**   ___**NOT from the selection**

I'll bet they'll be back someday.

___**from the selection**   ___**NOT from the selection**

Sue:
There were a few small swarms.

___**from the selection**   ___**NOT from the selection**

The last one died in 1902.

___**from the selection**   ___**NOT from the selection**

Nobody has seen one for over 100 years.

___**from the selection**   ___**NOT from the selection**

Try it. Answer the question below. Be sure to look back at the selection for the details you need to support your answer.

> **How did some families try to protect their gardens? Did it work?**

_____

_____

_____

_____

_____

_____

SLAMS—A Memory Gem

To help you remember the five rules in this chapter, remember this word: SLAMS!

 stands for **S**entence. Write your answers in complete sentences.

 stands for **L**ines. The number of lines on the answer sheet gives you an idea of how long your answer should be.

 stands for **A**nswer. Answer the question that the test asks. Answer all parts of the question. Read the question a few times to make sure you understand what the question asks.

 stands for **M**echanics. Mechanics are punctuation, capitalization, spelling, grammar, and usage. Your sentence mechanics should be correct. You should write without mistakes.

 stands for **S**upport. Remember to support your answer with details from the selection.

When you answer open-ended questions, try to recall this memory gem. Give your answers the *SLAMS* test. If your answer doesn't follow all of the *SLAMS* rules, fix it!

Remember—a good answer **SLAMS** the question!

Scoring Rubric

Every test has a different way of scoring the answers to an open-ended question. One of the most common methods is a scale of **0 to 4**. The **highest score is a 4**; the **lowest score is 0.**

It might help if you know what you need to get a **4** or a **3**. Here are some rubric guidelines for answering open-ended questions.

SCORE | **WHAT IT MEANS**

You answered the question clearly and completely.

You included ideas from the reading selection that are on target.

You supported these ideas with details and examples.

If the question asked you to, you connected the ideas from the reading selection to your own ideas and experiences.

You answered in complete and interesting sentences.

SCORE | **WHAT IT MEANS**

You answered the question.

You included some ideas from the reading selection.

You used some examples and details for support.

If the question asked you to, you connected some of the ideas from the reading selection to your own experiences.

Most of your sentences were complete.

SCORE | **WHAT IT MEANS**

You only answered part of the question.

You only included one or two ideas or details from the reading selection. The main ideas may not have been included.

You didn't connect your own ideas or experiences with the reading passage.

Many of your sentences were written incorrectly.

SCORE | **WHAT IT MEANS**

You didn't seem to understand the reading selection.

Your answer didn't include the important details from the selection.

You didn't connect your ideas to the reading passage.

You often wrote only single words or groups of words instead of complete sentences.

SCORE | **WHAT IT MEANS**

You didn't write anything; OR

You didn't answer the question asked.

Unit 1

Main Idea and Supporting Details

When you read, sentences usually appear in groups. Groups of sentences are called **paragraphs**.

Why does one paragraph end and another one begin? Each paragraph has a separate big idea. That idea is often called the **main idea**. The sentences in the paragraph are about that main idea. They **support** the main idea. That means the sentences explain or give important information about the main idea. This supporting information is called the **supporting details**.

A whole reading selection has a main idea, too. On a test, you might be asked to explain the main idea of a reading selection. Or you might be asked to identify the supporting details.

In this unit, you'll learn how to find the main idea and supporting detail.

18

Lesson 1

What Makes a Good Answer?

Read this short information article. The question on the next page asks you to tell about the main idea.

We All Scream for Ice Cream

The main idea is expressed in this paragraph.

Today, you might scream, I might scream, we all might scream for ice cream. Has everyone *always* screamed for this tasty treat? The answer, surprisingly, is yes!

People have been eating a form of ice cream for a very long time—nearly two thousand years. The first form of ice cream was snow or ice, topped with fruit or juice.

Hundreds of years later, people began adding cream to this cold, delicious treat. Everyone loved it, but it was not easy to make. The person making the ice cream had to beat and shake the creamy ingredients by hand for nearly an hour before the ingredients turned into ice cream. Another problem was that if it wasn't eaten right away, the ice cream would melt. Because it was so difficult to make and keep frozen, not many people got a chance to try ice cream.

The main idea is summed up in this paragraph, too.

Then freezers were invented! Machines in factories began making ice cream, and the freezers kept the ice cream cold. Grocery stores began selling packaged ice cream about a hundred years ago. Now everyone could experience this frozen delight, and ice cream soon zoomed to the top as people's favorite treat.

What is the main idea of this selection? Support your answer with details from the selection.

Marta's Answer:

Marta wrote a good answer to this question. Read what she wrote.

The main idea of this selection is that people have enjoyed ice cream for a long time. First, people ate snow or ice with fruit on it. Then they started mixing in cream. They had to make it by hand, so they couldn't make a lot. Finally, people began to make ice cream in factories and freeze it. Now everyone can eat ice cream.

What Makes Marta's Answer Work?

Marta does what the test scorers are looking for:

✓ She repeats part of the question to help focus her answer.

✓ She supports her answer with details from the selection.

✓ She writes her answer in complete sentences.

Let's take a closer look to see why Marta's answer would get a good score.

HINT!

The people who score the test look for the following things:

✳ A clear and complete statement of the main idea.

✳ Details from the selection that support your first sentence.

✳ Complete, correct, and interesting sentences.

1. Marta keeps her answer in focus by including part of the question in her answer. That helps her stick to the main topic.

   In which sentence does Marta answer the question? Write the sentence here.

   _____

   _____

   _____

2. In her answer, Marta gives details from the selection that support the main idea. One detail is that people ate snow or ice with fruit.

   In which sentence does Marta include this detail? Write the sentence here.

   _____

   _____

   _____

3. Marta includes not one but a few supporting details.

   Find another supporting detail in Marta's answer. Write the sentence here.

   _____

   _____

   _____

4. Marta ends her answer with a concluding sentence. This sentence sums up the main idea.

   What is Marta's conclusion? Write the sentence here.

   _____

   _____

   _____

Tools & Tips

Make sure you know the difference between a main idea and a supporting detail.

✓ The **main idea** is the BIG idea. It explains what all the details in the paragraph are about, put together.

✓ The **supporting details** are SMALLER bits of information. Details are facts, descriptions, and examples that explain the main idea.

Read the paragraph below.

> An American president helped make ice cream popular. James Madison was the fourth president of the United States. He had just been elected for the second time. His wife, Dolley, gave him a party at the White House. She served a brand-new dessert—ice cream. Soon, everyone wanted ice cream at their parties.

Which sentence states the main idea? Write it here.

_____

_____

Which sentences have supporting details? Write them here.

_____

_____

_____

_____

_____

Lesson 2

Revising and Improving a Weak Answer

Here is another reading passage. To answer the question that follows, you must find supporting details in the selection.

Who Invented the Ice Cream Cone?

No one knows for sure who first invented the ice cream cone. It may have been invented by a man named Italo Marciony. Other people, however, also claim to have invented the cone.

One such person was Ernest Hamwi. In 1904, he was selling waffles at the World's Fair in St. Louis. At another booth, a man was selling ice cream. The ice-cream seller ran out of dishes, and Hamwi offered him a waffle, twisted into a cone. It was the first ice cream cone—or was it?

> Look for a supporting detail in this paragraph.

Hamwi was not the only waffle-maker at the fair. Abe Doumar was also selling waffles, and a man next to him sold ice cream. That ice-cream seller also ran out of dishes, and he took a waffle from Abe Doumar. In fact, waffles and ice cream were both very popular at the fair. It is possible that other ice-cream sellers ran out of dishes and used waffles instead.

> More supporting details can be found in this paragraph.

Meanwhile, in New York City, Italo Marciony sold ice cream from a cart. He served his ice cream in glass dishes, but sometimes people dropped the dishes and broke them. Marciony began to serve the ice cream in paper cones. Then Marciony had another idea.

At the end of 1903, Marciony began baking waffles. He shaped the waffles into cups for ice cream. People loved eating the ice cream as well as the waffle cups. Was this the birth of the ice cream cone? No one knows for sure!

What reasons are given for why we don't know who invented the ice cream cone?

Kyle's Answer:

Kyle wrote an answer to this question, but it is not very good.

> There's more than one person. It might have been at the World's Fair in 1904. Another guy too with waffles.

Improving Kyle's Answer:

Kyle's answer would not get a good score because it is not complete. He says that there might be more than one person. He mentions a fair and waffles. But his answer is very short. He doesn't include enough supporting details from the selection. In addition, he doesn't always write complete sentences.

How could Kyle improve his answer? Use the questions below and on the next page to help you revise and improve Kyle's answer.

1. Kyle doesn't state the main idea completely.

   Check the question and the reading selection to see what else Kyle needs to add to his first sentence. Rewrite the first sentence here.

   _____

   _____

   _____

   _____

HINT!

The people who score the test look for the following things:

* A clear and complete sentence that tells the main idea.

* Details from the selection that **support** the main idea.

* Complete, correct, and interesting sentences.

2. Kyle mentions the World's Fair, but he doesn't say what happened there.

   Check the reading selection for the missing information. Write two new sentences of your own that support the main idea.

   _____

   _____

   _____

   _____

3. Kyle mentions another guy with waffles. Again, he doesn't give enough details. Who is the other guy? What about the waffles? Also, Kyle hasn't written a complete sentence.

   Look back at the reading selection to find the supporting details. Write two sentences that can replace what Kyle wrote. Make sure you write complete sentences.

   _____

   _____

   _____

   _____

4. **Now rewrite Kyle's answer here.**

   _____

   _____

   _____

   _____

   _____

   _____

   _____

   _____

   _____

HINT!

Make sure the answer meets all the **SLAMS** tests.

SCORE BUILDER

Before you forget—

What is the memory gem word?

_____

What does each letter stand for?

1 _____

_____

2 _____

_____

3 _____

_____

4 _____

_____

5 _____

_____

Lesson 3

Responding on Your Own

Here is another reading selection. The question that follows asks you to write a title for it. This kind of question is very much like a main-idea question. A good title expresses the main idea.

Look for the main idea in this first paragraph.

"Ow! Ow, ow, ow!" shrieked Lucy. "It's too cold. It hurts my teeth." In her hand she held an ice cream cone.

"Well, of course it's cold," her father said, enjoying his own ice cream. "It's ice cream, not hot cream."

"I know ice cream means it's cold," said Lucy, "but why can't it be less icy?"

"If ice cream were warmer, it wouldn't be as much fun to eat," her father said. "

"Why not?" Lucy asked, perplexed.

"Warm ice cream melts," her father explained.

"Hmmm," said Lucy. "Maybe we could put something on the ice cream to protect my teeth."

What supporting detail can you find in this paragraph?

Her father took out some crushed nuts and sprinkled them on Lucy's ice cream. "Try biting into the nuts first," he suggested.

Lucy tried, but the result was the same—her teeth still hurt.

"Instead of trying to change the ice cream," her father said, "let's change the way you eat it. Try licking the ice cream instead of biting it."

Very carefully, Lucy licked the ice cream. The ice cream sat cold and delicious on her tongue, but it didn't hurt her teeth. "That works!" she exclaimed.

Write a title for this story. Explain why your title is a good one. Include information from the story to explain your idea.

Write your answer on the lines below.

My Title

_____

_____

Why I Chose It

_____

_____

_____

_____

_____

_____

_____

_____

_____

_____

_____

_____

_____

_____

_____

_____

_____

HINT!

When you are finished, check your answer:

* Does your title tell what the selection is mainly about?

* What details from the selection support your title?

* Does your explanation meet all the SLAMS tests?

Reader's Response!
Revise & Edit

When you have finished writing about the selection, exchange papers with a partner. As you read each other's work, answer the questions below.

1 Did the writer fully answer BOTH parts of the question?   ___Yes ___ No
If not, what needs to be added or changed?
Write your response on the lines below.

_____

_____

2 Do you think the writer chose a good title?   ___ Yes ___ No
If you do, explain why. If you don't, explain why not.
Write your response on the lines below.

_____

_____

_____

3 Did the writer give clear reasons for his or her choice?   ___ Yes ___ No
If not, what needs to be added or changed?
Write your response on the lines below.

_____

_____

_____

4 Has the writer followed all the SLAMS rules?   ___ Yes ___ No
If not, which rules were not followed?
Check all the rules that apply.

S ___   L ___   A ___   M ___   S ___

5 **Give the paper back to your partner to revise and edit.**

Reviewing the Question

Questions about the main idea may be asked in different ways. Here are some of them. Pay special attention to the words in **dark type**.

- ◉ What is the **main idea** of this selection?

- ◉ What would be the **best title** for this story?

- ◉ What is this selection **mostly about**?

Questions about the supporting details may be asked in different ways, too. Here are some of them. Pay special attention to the words in **dark type**.

- ◉ Support your answer with **details from the selection**.

- ◉ **What** are the **reasons** you think so?

- ◉ Use **information from the story** in your explanation.

Comparison and Contrast

Look at the shapes below. How are the shapes alike?

Maybe you said that both shapes have straight lines, or both shapes have four sides. You are describing the shapes' **similarities**. You are describing the ways in which the shapes are *alike*. When you talk about how things are alike, you **compare** them.

Now explain how the two shapes are different. Maybe you said that one shape is bigger than the other, or that one shape is a rectangle and the other shape is a square. You are describing the shapes' **differences**. You are describing the ways that the shapes are *NOT alike*. When you talk about how two things are NOT alike, you **contrast** them.

In this unit, you will **compare** and **contrast** two characters in a story.

32

Lesson 4

What Makes a Good Answer?

Read this story about two friends named Flip and Elizabeth. The question that follows on the next page asks you to contrast them—to tell how they are different.

Flip Gets an Idea

Flip was daring me again.

"Don't be a chicken, Elizabeth," she said, shaking a finger at me. "We're both trying out for the school play. We're going to be Cinderella's ugliest and meanest stepsisters ever. It'll be great."

"Fine, fine, fine," I said. This was the fourth time today Flip had tried to convince me.

"Great. I already signed us up!" she said.

I sighed. Flip and I have been neighbors and best friends for our whole lives—nearly ten years—but we are really different. Flip is tall, with crazy curly red hair and green eyes. I am short, and I have straight brown hair and brown eyes. Flip is an only child, and she's always the center of attention. I have four brothers, and sometimes I feel like I never get noticed. Flip is brave, and she is always making me go along with her crazy ideas. I like to play it safe, but I do have fun when Flip drags me along on one of her adventures.

This time, the adventure was acting. Students from the fourth and fifth grades were trying out for *Cinderella*. "Everyone hates the ugly stepsisters, right?" said Flip. "But we'll make them funny. We'll make them trip and fall and snort and burp. Everyone will love it!"

Flip and I practiced every day at her house. We read the *Cinderella* script over and over again. Her mom rented old Cinderella movies for us to watch. On the day of the tryouts, we were definitely ready.

> *Dialogue can tell you a lot about a character.*

> *This paragraph is loaded with compare/contrast details.*

Elizabeth says that even though she and Flip have been best friends for ten years, they "are really different." How are Flip and Elizabeth different? Support your answer with details from the story.

Sam's Answer:

Sam wrote a good answer to this question. Read what Sam wrote. Then answer the questions that follow. The questions will help you understand how Sam wrote his answer.

One reason why Elizabeth says she and Flip are different is because they look different. The other way they are different is in their personalities. Flip is brave and adventurous, and she is used to being the center of attention. She's the one who signs them up for the play. It's also her idea to make the stepsisters funny. Elizabeth, however, is quiet. She says she likes to play it safe. She sometimes feels like she never gets noticed.

What Makes Sam's Answer Work?

Sam does what the test scorers are looking for:

✓ He reads the selection and the question carefully.
✓ He gives two ways in which they are different.
✓ He supports his ideas with details from the selection.
✓ He writes his answer in complete sentences.

Let's take a closer look to see why Sam's answer would get a good score.

1. Sam begins with one way Elizabeth and Flip are different.
   What is that reason? Write Sam's sentence here.

   _____

   _____

2. Sam then includes another way Elizabeth and Flip are different.
   What is that reason? Write Sam's sentence here.

   _____

   _____

3. Sam gives details from the selection that support this second reason.
   What does Sam write about Flip? Write Sam's sentences about Flip here.

   _____

   _____

   _____

   _____

4. After he describes Flip, Sam gives details that describe Elizabeth's personality.
   What does Sam write about Elizabeth? Write Sam's sentences about Elizabeth here.

   _____

   _____

   _____

   _____

Tools & Tips

When you compare and contrast, you use special words to point out similarities and differences. Sam does that in his answer:

Elizabeth, **however**, is quiet.

The word **however** tells the reader that Sam is going to describe how Elizabeth is **different** from Flip.

Here are some words you might use to compare and contrast.

To compare:	To contrast:
alike	but
also	different
and so	in contrast
both	not like
in the same way	unlike
like	on the other hand

Write a sentence in which you compare yourself to someone else. Use one of the comparison words or groups of words from the lists above.

_____

_____

_____

Lesson 5

Revising and Improving a Weak Answer

Read this selection. The question on the next page asks you to explain how Flip's personality changes. Notice that this question is also about differences.

A Change of Plans

Flip tried out first, then it was my turn. I read the lines for the stepsister perfectly, just as Flip and I had practiced.

"Great, Elizabeth," said Ms. Dobson. "Now I want you to read some of Cinderella's lines."

"But I want to be a stepsister with Flip," I said.

"We'll see," said Ms. Dobson. "Just try Cinderella."

After tryouts, Flip asked me how I did. "Even if you don't get to be a stepsister," said Flip, "you can still help me rehearse."

What is Flip like in this paragraph?

The next day, the parts were posted in the hallway. I had been chosen as Cinderella. Flip came up behind me and dropped her backpack. "Did we get it?" she asked. Then she read my name. "Oh," she said. "You're Cinderella?"

"I guess," I said. "Ms. Dobson made me read her part, even though I told her I wanted to be a stepsister."

"Yeah, right," said Flip. She started walking away.

"Wait, Flip," I said, but she didn't stop.

This paragraph has details about how Flip changes.

Flip didn't come over to my house that day, and she didn't call me after our favorite TV show. Play rehearsal started the next day. Flip had been cast as a stepsister along with LiLi Tay. She and LiLi were already sitting together when I came in.

"Hey, Flip," I said, but she didn't look up. During rehearsal, Flip and LiLi ignored me or whispered about me. I felt like I really was Cinderella with two mean stepsisters.

How does Flip's behavior toward Elizabeth change after she finds out that Elizabeth has the part of Cinderella? Support your answer with details from the story.

Yolanda's Answer:

Yolanda wrote an answer, but it would not get a good score.

> Flip doesn't act the same. She acts mad. And mean. Before she was nice.

Improving Yolanda's Answer

Yolanda's answer would not get a good score because it doesn't have enough information. She writes that Flip's behavior is different, and she describes her behavior in a very general way. Her answer doesn't include enough details from the selection to explain how Flip's behavior toward Elizabeth has changed. Yolanda also doesn't always write complete sentences.

How could Yolanda improve her answer? The questions that follow will help you revise and improve Yolanda's answer.

1. Yolanda doesn't have a clear and complete statement of her main idea. Her last sentence sounds like it should be part of her opening.

    Read Yolanda's last sentence. Then check the question to see what else Yolanda should write. Rewrite her first sentence here.

    _____

    _____

    _____

    _____

    _____

    _____

> **HINT!**
>
> The people who score the test look for the following things:
>
> ✳ A clear and complete sentence that describes how the character changes.
>
> ✳ Details from the selection that support your answer.
>
> ✳ Complete, correct, and interesting sentences.

2. Yolanda writes that Flip acts mad, but she doesn't give details to support this statement.

   What could Yolanda add to show that Flip acts mad? Rewrite this part of Yolanda's answer here.

   _____

   _____

   _____

3. Yolanda writes that Flip acts mean, but she doesn't give any details to support this statement. Also, this sentence is not complete.

   What could Yolanda add to show that Flip acts mean? Rewrite this part of Yolanda's answer here. Make sure all your sentences are complete.

   _____

   _____

   _____

4. **Rewrite Yolanda's entire answer here.**

   _____

   _____

   _____

   _____

   _____

   _____

   _____

   _____

   _____

HINT!

Make sure your answer meets all the SLAMS tests.

SCORE BUILDER

The SLAMS rules remind you that you need to write complete sentences. It's very easy, though, to do what Yolanda did and write a sentence that is not complete. Here's what Yolanda wrote:

She acts mad. And mean.

The group of words *And mean* look like a sentence. It starts with a capital letter and ends with a period, but it is not a complete sentence. It's a sentence **fragment**. Some words are missing.

You can correct a sentence fragment by adding the missing words: **She acts mean.**

You can also correct a sentence fragment by making it part of another sentence: **She acts mad and mean.**

Here is another sentence followed by a sentence fragment.

The stepsisters can be nasty. Or funny.

Correct the sentence fragment two ways.

1. **Add the missing words to make it a complete sentence.**

_____

_____

2. **Make the sentence fragment part of the first complete sentence.**

_____

_____

_____

Lesson 6

Responding on Your Own

Read this selection. This is the final part of the story about Flip and Elizabeth. The question that follows on the next page asks you to compare the two characters again.

Show Time!

Normally I wouldn't be excited about being in the spotlight, but I was excited about being Cinderella. My parents were really proud of me. Flip wasn't, and I was mad that Flip couldn't be happy for me. I was mad that she never gave me the chance to explain.

On the night of the play, I felt nervous. I could hear the people in the audience rustling, and I could feel the heat of the bright lights.

How are Flip and Elizabeth alike in this paragraph?

In the first scene, Flip was supposed to hand me a broom, but she tripped and crashed into me. We both fell down, the broom shot up in the air, and then it clattered to the stage. The audience was silent. Flip looked at me with big, round eyes.

"I'm sorry," I whispered.

She looked at me for a second more, then she started to laugh. I giggled, too. Then the whole audience joined in. We helped each other up, did a kind-of bow, then we got on with the show.

The next day, Flip and I talked about our fight.

"I was just so jealous," she said. "You didn't tell me that Ms. Dobson wanted you to be Cinderella."

Dialogue helps you learn how characters are alike.

"You never gave me a chance to explain," I said.

"I know," she said. "I'm sorry."

"I'm sorry, too," I said.

"You know what," she said. "I have this crazy idea...."

Even though they are different in many ways, Flip and Elizabeth are also alike. How are the two girls similar?

Write your answer on the lines below.

_____

_____

_____

_____

_____

_____

_____

_____

_____

_____

_____

_____

_____

_____

_____

_____

_____

_____

_____

HINT!

When you finish, check your answer.

* Have you identified at least two similarities between Flip and Elizabeth?

* Have you supported each similarity with details from the selection?

* Does your answer meet all the SLAMS tests?

Reader's Response!
Revise & Edit

When you have finished writing, exchange papers with a partner. As you read each other's work, answer the questions that follow:

1 Did the writer answer the question? ___Yes ___ No
Write your response here.

_____

_____

2 Did the writer name at least two similarities? ___ Yes ___ No
If not, what needs to be added or changed?
Write your response here.

_____

_____

3 Did the writer support each similarity with details? ___ Yes ___ No
If not, what needs to be added or changed?
Write your response here.

_____

_____

_____

4 Has the writer followed all the SLAMS rules? ___ Yes ___ No
If not, which rules were not followed?
Check all the rules that apply.

S ___   L ___   A ___   M ___   S ___

5 **Give the paper back to your partner to revise and edit.**

Reviewing the Question

Questions that ask you to compare and contrast may ask about these things:

- How two things are **alike**. Ways in which things are alike, or that things have in common, are called **similarities**.

- How two things are **different**. Ways in which things are different, or how things differ, are called **differences**.

- How two things are both **similar** and **different**.

If you see words like the ones below in **dark** type, the question is asking you to compare and contrast.

- How are Flip and Elizabeth **alike**?

- What do Flip and Elizabeth **have in common**?

- How do Flip and Elizabeth **differ** in their approach to the play?

- How does their friendship **change** from the beginning of the story to the end?

- In what ways are the beginning of the story and the end **similar**?

- How are the personalities of the two girls **different**?

Understanding Sequence

Read the numbers below. Each row forms a **sequence**.

1	2	3	4	5
5	10	15	20	25
6	5	4	3	2

Can you guess what the next number in each row should be? Recognizing the sequence helps you predict what might happen next.

Another word for *sequence* is *order*. When we talk about a sequence of events, we mean the order in which events and actions happen. Sequence is knowing what comes first, what comes next, and what comes last.

When you read, it is important to keep track of the sequence of events. When you write, it helps to arrange your ideas in the right order, too. It is easier for your reader to understand the sequence if you put them in the right order.

In this unit, you will work with sequence in directions and explanations.

Lesson 7

What Makes a Good Answer?

Read this recipe. The question on the next page asks you about the order of the steps.

Battercakes

My family thinks this recipe makes the best pancakes in the world. We call them "battercakes."

Dry Ingredients	Wet Ingredients
10 slices of bread	2 cups milk
1/2 cup all-purpose flour	1 stick (1/4 pound) butter
1 tablespoon baking powder	4 eggs
2 tablespoons sugar	

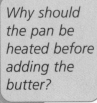

Look for a transition word in step 1.

1. Crumble the bread into a large mixing bowl. Add the flour, baking powder, and sugar. Then use a large spoon to mix everything evenly.

2. Pour the milk into another bowl. Make sure the bowl can be heated in a microwave oven. Add the stick of butter. Microwave the milk and butter until the butter has melted.

3. In another bowl, beat the four eggs with a fork.

4. Pour the milk, butter, and eggs over the dry ingredients. Stir with a spoon until everything is mixed evenly.

Why should the pan be heated before adding the butter?

5. Heat a large, flat griddle or frying pan. Set the flame at medium heat, or a little lower.

6. Smear butter on the griddle. It should melt right away.

7. Spoon the batter onto the griddle. Each spoonful will form a battercake, about 3 inches across.

8. When bubbles appear on the surface, flip over the battercakes. Remove them from the griddle after another half-minute or so.

> **When you make battercakes, what do you do with the dry ingredients? Support your answer with details from the reading selection.**

Jasmine's Answer:

Jasmine's answer to this question is a good one. Read what she wrote. Then answer the questions that follow. They will help you understand how Jasmine wrote her answer.

> When you make battercakes, you must first crumble up the bread into a big bowl. When the bread has been crumbled, you add the flour, sugar, and baking powder. Then you mix all the dry ingredients together with a big spoon.

What Makes Jasmine's Answer Work?

Jasmine does all the things the test scorers are looking for:

✓ She answers just the question that is asked—no more, no less.

✓ She gives the steps in an order that makes sense.

✓ She doesn't leave out any steps.

✓ She writes her answer in complete sentences.

Let's take a closer look to see why Jasmine's answer would get a good score.

1. Jasmine begins by stating the main idea of her answer. Notice that this helps Jasmine answer just the question that has been asked.

   What is the main idea? Write Jasmine's main-idea sentence here.

   _____

   _____

   _____

2. Then Jasmine gives the next step in the recipe.

   What is the next step? Write Jasmine's sentence here.

   _____

   _____

   _____

3. Jasmine then explains the next step for this part of the recipe.

   What is the next step? Write the next step here.

   _____

   _____

   _____

4. Jasmine uses transition words like *first* and *when*. These words make the order, or sequence, easy to follow.

   Find another transition word that Jasmine uses. Write the sentence here.

   _____

   _____

   _____

Tools & Tips

For certain kinds of writing, it is very important to explain things in the right sequence. Read the recipe below. Notice how confusing a recipe can be when the steps aren't in sequence:

How to Make Scrambled Eggs

You need to melt some butter in a pan. Make sure the pan is the right size to hold all the eggs you want to cook. So, before you do that, you need to decide how many eggs to cook. The eggs get all mixed up in a bowl before you cook them. But first, you need to crack open each egg and pour the egg into a mixing bowl. Then you beat the eggs until they have a lot of little air bubbles. Be careful not to get any eggshell in the bowl. Finally, pour the egg into the hot pan. Stir them while they are cooking. When they are soft and fluffy, and not wet, they are done.

On the paragraph above, number the steps that should come first, second, next, and so on. Visualize yourself or someone at home doing each step. What order makes sense? Then rewrite the directions on another sheet of paper.

Lesson 8

Revising and Improving a Weak Answer

Here is another reading passage. The question on the next page asks you about the plans for a party.

The Not-So Surprise Party

My two older sisters wanted to give our mom a surprise birthday party.

"That's great!" I said. "What do you want me to do?"

"Try to keep it a surprise," LuAnn said. At seventeen, she's the oldest, so she thinks she's the boss. Not only am I the youngest, I'm the only boy.

My other sister, Chrissie, jumped to my defense. "Hey, we need Jay's help. He's great with making cookies and stuff."

The details in this paragraph help answer the question.

"Fine," said LuAnn. "Mom's birthday is Friday. I'll ask to use the car that day so I have to pick her up at work." LuAnn just got her driver's license. "We'll get people to come early. As soon as I open the door, everyone should shout—"

"Surprise!" I said. LuAnn glared at me.

"I've got the invitations and the stamps," she continued, "and you two can fill them out. Use Mom's phone list. I'll do the shopping, and you two can fix the food."

We all got busy. On Friday, Chrissie and I put the food on the table and blew up the balloons, then it was time for LuAnn to pick up Mom.

Twenty minutes later our first guests arrived—LuAnn and Mom!

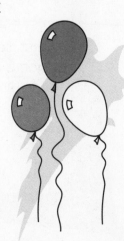

Events did not happen in the right order! What went wrong?

"Surprise," we mumbled.

"What happened?" hissed LuAnn. "Didn't you mail the invitations?"

"We gave them to you to mail because you had the car that day!" we both said.

Something went wrong with the plans for Mom's surprise party. What if nothing had gone wrong? What would have happened? Tell what would have happened, in the correct order. Use details from the selection and your own ideas.

Zachary's Answer:

Zachary wrote an answer to this question, but it would not get a good score.

> They would have had a surprise party.
> First Chrissie and Jay would fix the food.
> Then the guests would arrive. Their mother
> would be surprised.

Improving Zachary's Answer

Zachary's answer would not get a good score because it is not complete. He names some of the things that would have happened, but not all of them. In fact, he is missing some important steps—the things LuAnn, Chrissie, and Jay would have to do in order for the party to be a surprise.

How could Zachary make his answer more complete? Use the questions below and on the next page to help revise and improve Zachary's answer.

1. In his opening sentence, Zachary needs to state the main idea in more detail.

   What can Zachary add to make his opening sentence more complete? Rewrite Zachary's opening sentence here.

   _____

   _____

   _____

   _____

2. Zachary needs to include more details about preparing for the party, and he needs to put those details in the right order. A good place would be to put a sentence in between the first and second sentences.

What can Zachary add to make his description more complete? Write a new sentence for Zachary. Remember to use transition words to help the reader follow the sequence of events.

_____

_____

_____

_____

3. Zachary could also include more details before the last sentence.

What details could Zachary include here? Write one or two new sentences for Zachary.

_____

_____

_____

_____

4. **Rewrite Zachary's entire answer on the line below.**

_____

_____

_____

_____

_____

_____

_____

_____

HINT!

Make sure your answer meets all the SLAMS tests.

SCORE BUILDER

Zachary used two transition words in his answer: **first, then**. When you rewrote his answer, you might have added other transition words. Transition words help the reader follow the sequence of events.

What transition words did you use? Write them below.

_____

Share your transition words with a partner. What words did your partner use? If any of your partner's words were different, write them below.

_____

With your partner, come up with more transition words. See how many words you can think of that show order or sequence. The headings below will help you.

**Words That
Show Before**

_____

_____

**Words That Show
What's Next**

_____

_____

**Words That Show
What's First**

_____

_____

**Words That Show
What's Last**

_____

_____

Lesson 9

Responding on Your Own

Read the selection below. This time, you will read about the steps that turn a dinosaur into a fossil. On the next page, you will answer a question about the order of fossil-making steps.

How to Become a Fossil

Imagine for a moment that you are a dinosaur—a dinosaur with big plans. You want to become a fossil! You want your bones to end up in a museum, where human kids can see how big and strong you used to be. You have to plan ahead.

Look for transition words in the paragraph.

First, you must choose your last resting place. You need to find a place where your body will be covered with mud or sand as fast as possible. The bottom of a lake is a good place. So is a sandy desert or a shore near a river. If a lot of sand or mud piles up on your body—say, several thousand feet of it—then the sand or mud around your bones will be squeezed into rock.

Very slowly, water will dissolve some of the rock, like it dissolves salt or sugar. The water will soak into your bones, dropping tiny bits of dissolved rock into the spaces in your bones.

Over time, your original bones will disappear. A rock copy will remain in their place. You have become a fossil!

Can you count all six steps in this paragraph? They are in order!

Now you have to wait at least 65 million years. All that rock on top of you has to be worn away. If your luck holds, some human will spot your fossilized bones before they wear away, too. Scientists will dig up your bones. They will put your bones together again, and then you will stand, noble and proud, in a museum.

What happens to the dinosaur's bones in order for them to become a fossil? Use details from the selection to support your answer.

_____
_____
_____
_____
_____
_____
_____
_____
_____
_____
_____
_____
_____
_____
_____
_____
_____

HINT!

When you finish, check your answer.

* Have you included enough details to make your answer clear and complete?

* Are the details written in an order that makes sense?

* Have you used transition words to make the sequence easier for the reader to understand?

* Does your answer meet the SLAMS test?

Reader's Response!
Revise & Edit

When you have finished writing, exchange papers with a partner. As you read each other's work, answer the questions below.

1 Did the writer state the main idea clearly? ___Yes ___ No

2 Did the writer include enough details? ___Yes ___ No
If not, what needs to be added or changed?
Write your ideas here.

_____

_____

_____

3 Did the writer put the steps in an order that ___ Yes ___ No
makes sense? If not, what needs to be added or changed?
Write your ideas here.

_____

_____

_____

4 Did the writer use transition words? ___Yes ___ No

5 Has the writer followed all the SLAMS rules? ___ Yes ___ No
If not, which rules were not followed?
Check all the rules that apply.

S ___   L ___   A ___   M ___   S ___

6 **Give the paper back to your partner to revise and edit.**

Reviewing the Question

When you give someone directions or explain how to do something, sequence is important. When you explain how something happened, sequence is important. Sequence is even important when you tell a made-up story. The order of the events needs to make sense.

How can you tell when a question is asking about sequence? Here are some tips:

- The question might ask you to describe the steps in a process—how to make or do something.

- The question might ask you to retell what happened in all or part of a story.

- The question might ask you about a real event—what happened first, next, and last.

- The question might ask you to plan something—a party, a trip, a project.

Read the selection and answer the questions that follow.

Fourth Graders Throw a Party

Ms. Greenwald's class buzzed with excitement. School would be over soon, and they had a party to plan.

"I have an idea," Isabelle called out, waving her arm in the air.

"Me too, me too," said Anthony as his arm shot up.

"OK," said Ms. Greenwald. "Isabelle first, then Anthony."

Isabelle stood up and announced, "This is the way we should do it. We'll invite all our parents, and we'll decorate the classroom. We could make flowers and snowflakes out of paper. We could color them—the flowers, I mean."

Anthony interrupted. "No, let's not have it here, in the classroom. Let's go to the park. We'll have room to run around, and we won't have to make decorations. The park already has plenty of flowers and leaves."

"But what if it rains?" Isabelle asked. "If we stay here, it doesn't matter what the weather is like."

Anthony changed the subject. "What about food? Can we have pizza?"

"Wait a minute," said Ms. Greenwald. "The first thing we need to do is decide when to have the party. I suggest that we have it during lunchtime. Then we can serve sandwiches before dessert."

Everyone started shouting out ideas for food.

"Hold on," said Ms. Greenwald. "Monica, I'm putting you in charge of writing the food ideas on the board—sandwiches first. Then we can talk about dessert. When we have all the suggestions, we can vote on the food we want."

"Then can we vote on whether the party is in our classroom or in the park?" Anthony asked.

"Absolutely," said Ms. Greenwald. "Then we can all decide on a date and start making invitations."

1 Main Idea and Supporting Details

What is Isabelle's idea for the fourth-grade party? What reason does she give to support her plan? Use details from the selection in your answer.

_____

_____

_____

_____

_____

_____

_____

_____

2 Comparison and Contrast

How is Anthony's plan different from Isabelle's? Include details from the selection in your answer.

_____

_____

_____

_____

_____

_____

_____

_____

3 Understanding Sequence

Imagine that your class is planning a party. What would you need to do first? What would you do second? Use details from the selection, as well as your own ideas, to explain your plan.

_____

_____

_____

_____

_____

_____

_____

_____

_____

Reading What Is on the Page

As a reader, you have many jobs. First, you need to know what information is included in the selection. This is called **reading what is on the page**.

- You need to know the *main idea*.

- You need to know the *details* the author has included.

When test-makers want to know if you understand what is on the page, they often ask you to explain the details. The questions ask you to explain only the information given. When you answer an open-ended question about what is on the page, you show how well you understand what you have read.

In this unit, you will read a selection about how crows make tools. Then you will answer some questions that test how well you can describe what the crows do.

Lesson 10

What Makes a Good Answer?

Read the true story about crows below. After you read, answer the questions that test how well you can explain what you have read.

The Clever Crows of New Caledonia

Look for the main idea in this paragraph.

New Caledonia is a tropical island in the South Pacific, about 800 miles east of Australia. Crows live on the island, but they are no ordinary crows. These crows make tools! The people of New Caledonia are proud of their clever crows. They even put a crow picture on one of their stamps.

Why would crows need tools? They need tools to get their food! The crows of New Caledonia eat insect grubs. These grubs live deep in small holes in tree branches. The holes are too small for a crow's beak to fit inside. So the crows make tools to get the grubs.

One kind of tool they make is from a twig. The crows bend the tip of the twig. Then they poke the tip into the hole and fish out the grubs.

Look for two examples of tools.

A more clever tool is made from a leaf. The crows choose the leaves from a tree called the pandanus. They choose these leaves because the leaves are very long and stiff.

To start, the crows nip the side of a leaf with their beaks, making a small tear. Then they rip off a long strip from the leaf. This strip will be the tool. They finish off the tool by nipping off the end of the strip. The finished tool is perfect for poking into holes and spearing grubs. This process is called the nip-and-rip method.

This tool, however, has a problem. Sometimes the leaf is too long and thin. It bends and breaks if the crow pokes too hard with it. The New Caledonia crows have figured out a way to solve this problem. Most of the crows now make a fancier tool. They nip and rip the leaf, forming steps. The leaf-tool is thin at one end, then it gradually gets fatter.

This tool is nearly perfect. It can still poke into small holes, but it won't bend and break so easily.

Scientists from around the world have come to New Caledonia to study the clever crows. They observe the crows' tool-making methods, but there's still a lot more to learn. Scientists haven't figured out how the crows know how to make tools. Is tool-making a part of being a crow, just as web-making is part of being a spider? Or do crows learn by watching other crows? Do mother and father crows teach their young how to make tools?

The New Caledonia crows are very clever. Are crows that live near you clever, too? Watch the crows where you live. Observe if they make tools to help them get food, like the New Caledonia crows.

How does this information support the main idea?

One sentence here sums up the main idea.

Notice that the instructions below ask you to use details from more than one part of the selection.

> **Describe the ways that the New Caledonia crows get their food. Use details from the whole selection to support your answer.**

Clyde's Answer:

Here is Clyde's answer. Read what Clyde wrote. Then answer the questions that follow to see what makes Clyde's answer a good one.

The New Caledonia crows have a special way to get their food. They know how to make tools. They use their tools to get insect grubs out of tree branches.

The tree branches have small holes. The insect grubs live inside these holes. The crows' beaks are too big to reach into these holes. So the crows need to find another way to get to the insect grubs.

The New Caledonia crows make different kinds of tools for getting insect grubs. They make one tool out of a twig. They can bend the end of the twig. Then they use it to get into the holes and dig out the grubs.

Another kind of tool is made from a leaf. The crows bite the leaf and tear it to make a kind of spear. They can stick the end of the leaf into a hole and get the grubs out that way. The New Caledonia crows are very clever.

What Makes Clyde's Answer Work?

Clyde's answer includes the things that test scorers look for:

✓ A first paragraph that states the main idea.

✓ Two good examples to support the main idea.

✓ A clear, detailed description of what the crows do and why.

✓ A good closing sentence.

Now take a closer look at Clyde's answer to see what makes it work.

1. Clyde begins his answer by stating the main idea. Notice that he includes part of the question in his answer.

   What is Clyde's main-idea sentence? Write it here.

   _____

   _____

   _____

2. In his second paragraph, Clyde gives the reason that the crows use tools to get their food.

   What is that reason? Write the sentence that expresses the reason here.

   _____

   _____

   _____

3. Clyde gives two examples of the ways the crows use tools to get their food. The first example, in paragraph 3, explains that the crows use sticks. The second example is in paragraph 4.

   What is that example? Write the sentence that introduces the example on the lines below.

   _____

   _____

   _____

4. Clyde includes details from the selection about the way the crows make and use their tools. For example, he writes that the crows bend the end of a twig to use as a tool.

What other details does Clyde give? Write about the details in your own words.

_____

_____

_____

_____

_____

5. Clyde ends, or closes, his answer with a sentence that sums up what he's learned about the New Caledonia crows.

What is Clyde's closing sentence? Write it here.

_____

_____

_____

HINT!

Clyde's closing sentence also appears in the reading selection!

Tools & Tips

When you explain **how** something is done or **how** something works, you can improve your answer by also explaining **why**. Clyde did this when he wrote:

> *The crows' beaks are too big to reach into these holes.*

He explained **why** the crows needed another way to get the insect grubs.

Try it! First, pick a task or a process. Make sure the task is something you know how to do. Here are some ideas to get you started:

- ✓ how to make a sandwich
- ✓ how to play soccer
- ✓ how to care for a pet
- ✓ how to ride a bike

Next, think about *how* you do this task. Write a sentence that explains one step in the process.

_____

_____

Now think of *why* you do this step. Write a sentence that explains *why* this step is needed.

_____

_____

68

Lesson 11

Strategy: Finding Details

Clyde's answer works because he included details from the selection. The details helped him answer the question clearly and completely.

How can you find the details you need to answer an open-ended question? Here are some things you can do:

✓ Make sure you know the *main idea*.

✓ Ask yourself *questions* about the selection.

✓ Look for *clues* in the selection that will help you answer your own questions.

Try it with this paragraph.

> Chess is a tough game. Players don't knock each other down, the way they do in football. They don't have to run fast or jump high. They just have to think very hard. Chess is played on a board. In order to win, each player needs to figure out what the other one might do next—or even four turns from now. Players set traps for each other. They attack each other's pieces and try to capture them. Even with all this action, the players sit down the whole time.

1. Make sure you know the main idea.

   Write the main idea of this paragraph on the lines below.

   _____

   _____

   _____

HINT!

You can usually find the main idea at or near the beginning of the selection.

2. Ask yourself questions about the main idea. For example, one question you might ask is: Why is chess a tough game?

Think of another question you might ask. Write your question below.

_____

_____

3. Look for clues in the selection that answer your question.

Write the answer to your question below.

_____

_____

4. Find other details to make your answer more complete.

Write your details, in complete sentences, below.

_____

_____

_____

_____

5. Now try it on your own. Read the paragraph below. In your own words, tell what the paragraph is mainly about.
Write your answer on another sheet of paper.

Checkers is a fun and easy game to play. Two players are needed. One player takes the black checkers, and the other player takes the white or red checkers. Players set up their checkers on opposite ends of the board. Then players slide their checkers across the board to reach the other side. If one player's checker jumps over the other player's checker, the player takes that checker and keeps it. The winner is the player who still has checkers on the game board.

HINT!

These questions can help you write your answer:

* What is the main idea?

* How many players are needed?

* What do the players do?

* Why does a player jump over another player's checker?

* How does a player win the game?

Lesson 12

Revising and Improving a Weak Answer

In this lesson, you are going to use what you've learned to improve an answer that is not successful. Look again at the selection *The Clever Crows of New Caledonia*. The question below asks you to find information in the selection.

> **How do the New Caledonia crows turn leaves into tools? Use information from the text to support your answer.**

Megan's Answer:

Here is Megan's answer.

> They bite the leaves. They tear them, too.
> Then they can poke the leaf into a hole.

Improving Megan's Answer

Megan has answered the question in a very general way.

✓ They bite the leaves.

✓ They tear the leaves.

She also gives one reason the crows bite and tear the leaves:

✓ Then they can poke the leaf into a hole.

But Megan has not explained completely how the crows turn the leaves into tools. She needs to describe more fully the steps the crows follow. She also needs to state her main idea more clearly.

Imagine that you wrote Megan's answer. Ask yourself the following questions to help you revise and improve it.

1. Have I stated the main idea? How can I use the question to help me state the main idea?

   Write a new opening sentence here.

   _____

   _____

   _____

2. Have I written enough to answer the question? What details should I add to explain how the crows bite and tear the leaves?

Write a new explanation here.

_____

_____

_____

_____

3. Have I said enough to answer the question? What details can I add to explain why the crows bite and tear the leaves?

Write a sentence or two with details here.

_____

_____

_____

_____

4. Have I written a good closing sentence? Does my closing sum up the main idea?

Write a closing sentence here.

_____

_____

_____

_____

HINT!

Make sure your answer meets all the SLAMS tests.

5. **Rewrite Megan's answer on another sheet of paper.**

SCORE BUILDER

To make sure you've stated the main idea in your answer, include part of the question in your opening sentence. Clyde did this in his answer. The question was:

Describe the ways that the New Caledonia crows get their food. Use details from the whole selection to support your answer.

Clyde's opening sentence is below. Notice the words that are <u>underlined</u>. These words appear in the question.

<u>The New Caledonia crows</u> have a
special <u>way to get their food</u>.

Try it! Use your own words to write another main-idea sentence for the question above. Remember to use some words from the question in your sentence.

_____

_____

_____

_____

Responding on Your Own

Here is one more question about the clever crows of New Caledonia. This time you will answer on your own, without models or questions to help you. Plan your answer carefully. Think about what you have learned from studying Clyde's answer and improving Megan's answer. You should also use the following things to help you write your answer:

✓ the **strategy** you have practiced (finding details)

✓ the tips you were given in **Tools & Tips**

✓ the reminders in the **Score Builder**

> **What problem did the New Caledonia crows have with their leaf tools? How did they solve this problem? Support your answer with details from the reading selection.**

Write your answer on the lines below.

_____

_____

_____

_____

_____

_____

_____

_____

_____

_____

_____

_____

_____

HINT!

Remember that the test scorers will be looking for the following things:

* An opening that states your main idea.

* A description of the problem.

* An explanation of how the crows have solved the problem.

* A clear closing sentence.

Reader's Response!
Revise & Edit

When you have finished writing, exchange papers with a partner. As you read each other's work, answer the questions below.

1 Did the writer answer both parts of the question?   ___Yes ___ No

2 Did the writer state the main idea clearly?   ___ Yes ___ No
Explain your answer.
Write your response here.

_____

_____

_____

3 Did the writer use supporting details?   ___ Yes ___ No
If not, what needs to be changed?
Write your response here.

_____

_____

_____

4 Did the write include a closing sentence?   ___ Yes ___ No

5 Has the writer followed all the SLAMS rules?   ___ Yes ___ No
If not, which rules were not followed?
Check all the rules that apply.

S ___   L ___   A ___   M ___   S ___

6 **Give the paper back to your partner to revise and edit.**

Reviewing the Question

A question that asks you to explain what is on the page can be written in different ways. Here are some of them. Pay special attention to the words in **dark type**.

- **How** do crows make tools?

- **What** do the crows do with twigs and leaves?

- **What** have scientists learned by studying crows?

- **Where** do crows like to live?

- **When** do crows need tools?

Notice that these questions all have something in common. They all contain question words. Question words point to information in the selection that helps answer the question.

Pay attention to the question words when you read an open-ended question. The question words usually mean that you need to find information that is stated directly on the page.

Reading Between the Lines

Sometimes open-ended questions ask you to read "between the lines." For these questions, you must apply a special kind of thinking. You need to **make inferences**. When you make inferences, you combine information in the text with things you already know to come up with a new idea.

For example, suppose you read the following sentence:

A burning smell drifted through the air, and smoke billowed from the frying pan.

How would you answer this question: *What do you think happened?*

The answer is not on the page. Instead, you combine the facts you do have—burning smell, smoke, frying pan—with your own knowledge:

Someone has burned the food.

You have made an inference. You figured out the answer by combining information on the page with what you know. You read *between* the lines.

In this unit, you will practice reading between the lines.

Lesson 14

What Makes a Good Answer?

Read the story below. The open-ended questions that follow ask you to read "between the lines." You will make inferences to explain what happens in the story and why.

Full House

The music stopped, and fifty young dancers caught their breath.

"Good job," the director said. "Now get some rest."

Soon the stage was empty, except for one girl. Natalie didn't want to leave. She walked slowly to the curtain, still hearing the music in her mind. Her arms and hands moved to the silent melody. Touching the velvet curtain, she peeked out and saw all the empty seats. The seats filled the hall, all the way to the top balcony. The audience had yet to arrive, and the huge, dark theater seemed to grow bigger and bigger.

Natalie's knees began to shake. Her stomach flip-flopped. She felt hot. She felt cold. She felt her hand slipping down the curtain. She didn't feel herself falling until strong arms began to lift her up.

Why might your knees shake and your stomach flip-flop?

"Drink this, slowly," the director said, giving her a sip of water. He helped her stand, then pointed to the empty hall. "Those seats may look frightening now, but they are not."

"I don't understand," Natalie said, puzzled.

"Natalie, I want you to close your eyes," he said. "Imagine the hall is filled with every dancer who ever danced here. Seated in the front rows are all the children who have danced your part. They are all here to welcome you. Tonight, you will be one of them."

Natalie opened her eyes, took a deep breath, and stood up, tall and straight. She looked at the empty seats and smiled. Once more the music played in her mind. Her knees no longer shook, and her stomach remained calm.

Why do you think Natalie's knees begin to shake and her stomach flip-flops? Use details from the story in your answer.

Margo's Answer:

Here is Margo's answer. Read what she wrote. Then answer the questions that follow to see why her answer is a good one.

Natalie's knees shake and her stomach flip-flops because she is nervous. When she peeked through the curtain, she saw all those empty seats. The theater looked so big and empty. She could see seats all the way to the top balcony.

Natalie is probably thinking about all those seats filled with people. She becomes nervous thinking about dancing in front of all those filled seats. She might be afraid to dance with so many people watching her. All these thoughts make Natalie nervous, so her knees shake and her stomach flip-flops.

What Makes Margo's Answer Work?

Margo includes all the things the test scorers look for:

✓ A statement of her main idea.

✓ An explanation of Natalie's feelings, showing that Margo has read between the lines.

✓ Details from the selection to support her answer.

✓ Clear and complete sentences.

Now take a closer look at Margo's answer to see what makes it work.

1. Margo begins her answer by stating the main idea.

   What is Margo's main idea? Write the main-idea sentence here.

   _____

   _____

   _____

2. In the first paragraph, Margo gives details to explain her main idea.

   What details does Margo include? Write one of Margo's details here.

   _____

   _____

   _____

3. Margo supports her main idea in the second paragraph, too.

   What example does Margo give in the second paragraph to support her main idea? Write the example here.

   _____

   _____

   _____

4. Margo reads between the lines to answer the question. She sums up her answer in her closing sentence.

   Write Margo's closing sentence here.

   _____

   _____

   _____

Tools & Tips

In the story *Full House*, not everything is explained to you. You know the characters' actions and you hear what they say, but you need to "read the between the lines" to fully understand what is happening. Questions like the ones below can help you.

✓ Why did she do that?

✓ Why did he sound that way?

✓ Why did she say that?

✓ Why did he feel that way?

✓ Why might I act this way or say these things?

Here's another question about the story:

Why did Natalie stay on the stage when the other dancers left?

Read the details from the story below. Put a check mark next to the detail that best helps answer the question.

__ **a.** Natalie still heard the music in her mind.

__ **b.** The director said they had done a good job.

On another sheet of paper, explain your choice.

Lesson 15

Strategy: Finding Clues

Reading between the lines means combining clues in the selection with your own knowledge.

For example, read these paragraphs:

> "Oh, no!" laughed their mother as Andrew and April came in the back door. The two children had big grins on their mud-streaked faces. Their sneakers left big muddy footprints on the steps.

> "I guess it can't be helped at this time of year," their mother said, handing them a towel.

Why do you think Andrew and April are so muddy?

The answer doesn't appear in the text. Instead, you must look for clues and think about what you know.

Here's one clue:

Their mother laughed.

This clue tells you that nothing bad has happened. Their mother was not upset. She thought Andrew and April looked funny.

Now let's look for another clues. Read the sentences below. Which sentence helps you answer the question?

__ **a.** April and Andrew came in the back door.

__ **b.** Their mother said, "It can't be helped at this time of year."

Sentence **a** is *NOT* a good choice. It's true that April and Andrew came in the back door, but that detail doesn't tell you why they are muddy.

Sentence **b** is a better choice. This clue tells you that the mud probably has something to do with the weather. Maybe it's been raining hard, or maybe snow and ice have melted. Your own knowledge about the weather helps you recognize sentence **b** as a good clue.

Here are two more short selections. Each one is followed by a question and two possible clues to help you answer the question. Put a checkmark next to the clue that can help you answer the question.

1. Jordan couldn't stop smiling when he heard the crowd cheer. It didn't matter that he was hot and sweaty. He ran as fast as he could. He had already passed third base, and the crowd was shouting his name.

What has just happened in this story?

CLUES to help answer the question:

__ **a.** Jordan has already passed third base.

__ **b.** Jordan is hot and sweaty.

2. Frowning, Tonya looked at the question. Her teacher walked quietly around the room. All the other students were writing as fast as they could. Tonya held her pencil tightly, but her paper was still blank.

What is the matter with Tonya?

CLUES to help answer the question:

__ **a.** Tonya's teacher walks quietly around the room.

__ **b.** Tonya's paper is still blank.

Lesson 16

Revising and Improving a Weak Answer

Now you are ready to try improving an answer that is *not* successful. Look again at the story *Full House*. Then read the question below. Notice that the question asks you to explain both *how* and *why* Natalie's feelings change.

> **Natalie's knees began to shake and her stomach to flip-flop after she peeked out from behind the curtain. Then her feelings changed. How and why did they change? Use details from the story to explain your answer.**

Scott's Answer:

Here is the answer Scott wrote. Read it carefully. Then use the questions that follow to help you revise and improve his answer.

> Natalie felt sick because she saw all the empty seats. The director gave her a drink of water. He talked to her. That made her feel better.

Improving Scott's Answer

Scott wrote part of an answer:

✓ He gives one reason why Natalie felt sick.

✓ He states two things that the director did to make her feel better.

Scott's answer, however, is too short, and it doesn't show that Scott can read between the lines. His answer needs to include more details about why Natalie reacted like she did and how the director helped her to feel better.

Answer the following questions to help revise and improve Scott's answer.

1. Has Scott given enough details to explain why Natalie's knees shake and her stomach flip-flops?

   What other details can Scott add? Write them here.

   _____

   _____

   _____

2. Has Scott explained what the director said when he talked to her?

   Write details about the director here.

   _____

   _____

   _____

   _____

3. Has Scott explained why the director's words help Natalie?

   Write why on the lines below.

   _____

   _____

   _____

   _____

4. Has Scott written a good sentence to end, or close, his answer?

   Write a sentence to help Scott sum up his ideas.

   _____

   _____

   _____

   _____

SCORE BUILDER

One way to improve your score on an open-ended question is to write your answers in clear, complete sentences. For example:

> **The enormous white bear stood on its hind legs. With a roar, the bear threw itself into the icy water and began to swim.**

What makes these sentences clear and complete?

✓ Each sentence mentions exactly **who** the sentence is about.

✓ Each sentence describes exactly **what** happens.

✓ Each sentence starts with a capital letter and ends with a period.

✓ Each sentence has a subject (the bear) and a predicate (or action).

Find one detail in the sentences that tells **who** the sentences are about. **Write it here.**

_____

_____

Find one detail in the sentences that tell **what** happens. **Write it here.**

_____

_____

Responding on Your Own

Now you are going to answer another question about the story *Full House*. This time, you will answer the question on your own, without models or questions to help you. As you plan and write your answer, think about what you have learned from studying Margo's answer and improving Scott's answer. You should also use the following things to help you write your answer:

✓ **the strategy** you have practiced (finding clues and applying what you know about those clues)

✓ the tips you were given in **Tools & Tips**

✓ the reminders in the **Score Builder**

Notice that this question, like the first two, asks you to read between the lines and explain something that may not be stated directly in the story.

> **Why does the director tell Natalie about past dancers sitting in the audience? Include details from the story as well as things you know in your answer.**

Write your answer on the lines below.

_____

_____

_____

_____

_____

_____

_____

HINT!

The test scorers will look for the following things:

✳ A statement of the main idea.

✳ Supporting details from the story.

✳ An explanation of things that are not in the story.

✳ Clear and complete sentences.

_____

_____

_____

_____

_____

Reader's Response!
Revise & Edit

When you have finished writing, exchange papers with a partner. As you read each other's work, answer the questions below.

1   Did the writer answer the question?   ___Yes ___ No

2   Did the writer include details from the story?   ___Yes ___ No
If yes, which details? If no, which details
would have helped?

Write your response here.

_____

_____

_____

3   Did the writer include his/her own knowledge?   ___Yes ___ No
If yes, what? If no, what could the writer
have included?

Write your response here.

_____

_____

_____

4   Has the writer followed all the SLAMS rules?   ___ Yes ___ No
If not, which rules were not followed?

Check all the rules that apply.

S ___   L ___   A ___   M ___   S ___

5   **Give the paper back to your partner to revise and edit.**

Reviewing the Question

A question about reading between the lines can be asked in many ways. Here are a few you might find. Pay special attention to the words in **dark** type.

- **What do you think** Natalie was feeling in the beginning of the story?

- **Why do you think** Natalie is so nervous?

- **What do you think** Natalie was feeling at the end of the story?

- **Why do you think** the director told Natalie to imagine other dancers in the theater?

- **What do you think** the director meant when he said, "Tonight you will be one of them"?

Notice that these questions all begin with **what do you think** or **why do you think**. Watch for words like these in an open-ended question. They are usually a clue that you are not going to find the information on the page. Instead, you are going to have to read between the lines.

Reading Beyond the Lines

A third kind of reading involves **reading beyond the lines**. This means understanding how a reading selection connects to real life. Readers who can read beyond the lines think about what they have learned from the selection and consider how to apply it to their own experiences.

An open-ended question can ask you to make connections between the reading selection and your own life. You might need to go beyond what you've read and make a connection with something that has happened to you. Or you might need to state your opinion on the topic or explain your ideas.

As you read the next selection, think about what you already know about the topic. Also, think about your own experiences and feelings. You will need to include some of these things in your answers to the open-ended questions in this unit.

Lesson 18

What Makes a Good Answer?

Read the selection below. As you read, think about your own school.

Fit for Life

The music blasts, and 25 fourth graders leap and spin. For 35 minutes, they pour all their energy into dancing. They don't stop until the bell rings and class is over.

> Look for details about the King School gym class.

This gym class at King School is unlike many gym classes. Students in this class don't spend time learning the rules of a team sport, or standing around watching while only a few students run, leap, or catch the ball. Instead, every single student is active from the minute class begins. Also, many schools often have gym only every other day. The students at King School have gym five days a week.

These students are not trying to win a game, but they do have goals. One goal is to become fit, to become strong, to stretch easily, and to have energy. Another goal is to be fit for life. In order to be fit for life, they must learn the kinds of exercises that they will be able to do all their lives.

The students at King School have a third goal, too. They would like to win the President's Challenge. The President's Challenge is part of the President's Council on Physical Fitness and Sports. The Council was set up in 1966 to encourage more Americans to exercise. The Council explains that everyone—children and adults—needs to exercise at least half an hour a day, five days a week. By exercise, the Council means a real workout—running or walking very fast.

The Council has found that almost half the adults in this country don't exercise at all. More than half of the people who do exercise don't do it very often.

Exercise is very important, but not everyone exercises as much as they should. Below are some key points about exercise, childhood, and school gym classes.

- Exercise is important for health. It helps the body to run smoothly. It can help prevent many diseases.

- People need to start being active when they are young. This is the best way to continue to be active and fit as adults.

- Most children have gym class in school only once or twice a week. In these gym classes, a hard, heart-thumping workout is usually less than twenty minutes.

Lists often give you good details.

For these reasons, some schools are changing their gym classes. The gym classes meet five days a week. Students might dance, run, juggle, climb rocks, or do yoga, all activities that students can do on their own. They don't need a team in order to exercise. Gym teachers hope kids will take these exercises into adulthood.

So why should you put down your video game or turn off your TV? Why should you start skating or riding a bike instead? If you're going for the President's Challenge, you could win a prize for yourself or your school. To win the prize, you need to be able to run and to demonstrate strength and flexibility.

The main idea is often retold in the last paragraph.

The biggest prize of all, however, is that by exercising regularly, you will feel better and enjoy life more—as a child and as an adult.

Do you think you are physically fit? Why or why not? Include details from the selection to help explain your answer.

Terrell's Answer:

Read what Terrell wrote. Then answer the questions that follow to see why Terrell's answer is a good one.

I think I am physically fit. I am very strong and can run very far. The President's Council on Physical Fitness and Sports says you need to be able to do these two things. I also think I am fit because we have gym class every day in our school. In class, we do some of the things the selection talks about. We run and dance. We also stretch our backs and legs every day.

Another reason I think I am fit is that I like to be active outside of school. After school and on weekends, I play outside. I ride my bicycle around the neighborhood. If other kids are around, we might play softball or soccer. I hope I get in-line skates for my birthday. Then I'll play street hockey, too. Most of the time, I like these things better than TV.

What Makes Terrell's Answer Work?

Terrell's answer includes the things that the test scorers look for:

✓ A clear statement of his opinion.

✓ Two good reasons that include details from the selection.

✓ Examples from his own life that support the reasons.

✓ Clear and complete sentences.

Now take a closer look at Terrell's answer to see what makes it work.

1. Terrell begins by stating his opinion. Notice that this is the main idea of his answer.

   What is Terrell's opinion? Write the sentence in which Terrell states his opinion here.

   _____

   _____

   _____

2. In both paragraphs, Terrell includes details that are connected to the reading selection.

   What are some of these details? Write a detail from paragraph 1 here.

   _____

   _____

   _____

   Write a detail from paragraph 2 here.

   _____

   _____

   _____

3. In both paragraphs, Terrell also includes examples from his own life.

   What are some of these examples? Write an example from paragraph 1 here.

   _____

   _____

   _____

   Write an example from paragraph 2 here.

   _____

   _____

   _____

4. Terrell's sentences are all clear and complete.

   Find an example of a clear and complete sentence that Terrell has written. Write the sentence here.

   _____

   _____

   _____

Tools & Tips

Some open-ended questions ask about things that have happened to you. The questions ask you to connect what you've read with your own experience. That's the kind of question Terrell just answered.

Notice what Terrell did when he answered this question:

✓ He included details about his own experience.

✓ He made these details into a story about himself.

He could have just listed the details, like this:

> I ride my bicycle. I play softball or soccer. I might play street hockey.

Instead, he made the details part of a story.

> After school and on weekends, I play outside. **I ride my bicycle** around the neighborhood. If other kids are around, we might **play softball or soccer**. I hope I get in-line skates for my birthday. Then I'll **play street hockey,** too. Most of the time, I like these things better than TV.

Which answer do you think is more interesting to read? When you answer open-ended questions, try to make your writing flow naturally, as if you are telling a story about yourself.

Lesson 19

Strategy: Making Connections

When an open-ended question asks you to read beyond the lines, it usually asks you to connect your own experience or ideas to the reading selection. Kelly read the same selection that Terrell did. When she read the following paragraph, she was looking for ideas she could connect to. As a result, she paid special attention to certain words. To help you see these words, we've put them in **dark type** below:

> The students at King School have a third goal, too. They would like to win the President's Challenge. The President's Challenge is part of the President's Council on Physical Fitness and Sports. The Council was set up in 1966 to encourage more Americans to exercise. **The Council explains that everyone—children and adults—needs to exercise at least half an hour a day, five days a week.** By exercise, the Council means a real workout—running or walking very fast.

The words in dark type made Kelly think about how much she exercised. She realized that she had gym five days a week. She also realized that her gym class exercised very hard for more than half an hour. Read Kelly's answer below.

The President's Council on Physical Fitness says that everybody should exercise hard five days a week. It says that we should exercise for at least half an hour each time. In our school, we have gym five days a week, and the class is forty minutes long.

1. Which part of Kelly's answer came from the reading selection?
   Write those sentences here.

_____

_____

_____

_____

2. Which part of Kelly's answer came from her own experience?
Write that sentence here.

_____

_____

_____

Here is a paragraph from a different reading selection:

> "Children need more chances to get exercise," says Dr. Stefanie Farber. "That's why County College has set up an after-school and weekend program." Children between the ages of five and ten will be able to swim in the college pool. They will also be able to play soccer at the college. They can take dance classes or learn gymnastics, too.

3. Which words or sentences have ideas that you can connect to?
Write them here.

_____

_____

_____

_____

4. How would you connect these words or sentences to your own ideas or experiences?
Write some sentences about your own ideas or experiences here.

_____

_____

_____

_____

Here is one more reading selection:

In the new physical education programs, more kids can have fun in gym class. They don't need to be great athletes. They don't need to hit home runs or score winning goals. Instead of trying to beat someone else, each student can just try to do his or her best. Maybe the students can run a little faster or jump a little higher than they did before. They're doing something that's good for them, and they feel good about themselves, too.

5. Which words or sentences contain ideas that you can connect to?
   Write them here.

   _____

   _____

   _____

   _____

6. How would you connect these words or sentences to your own ideas or experiences?
   Write some sentences about your own ideas or experiences here.

   _____

   _____

   _____

   _____

   _____

Revising and Improving a Weak Answer

Now that you know what a good answer looks like, you can try to improve an answer that isn't quite as good. Look again at the reading selection *Fit for Life*. Read the question below. It asks you to read beyond the lines.

> **What does it mean to be "fit for life"? Think of someone you know who is a good example of being fit for life. Explain what he or she does to be fit for life.**

Mia's Answer:

Read Mia's answer below. Then use the questions that follow to help you revise and improve Mia's answer.

> My big sister is a good example. She exercises a lot. And she's a very fast runner.

Improving Mia's Answer

Mia has the beginning of an answer.

✓ She has named someone who is a good example of "fit for life."

✓ She has named two things that this person does to be fit.

This is just the start. Mia needs a more complete statement of her main idea. She needs to include some details from the reading selection. She also needs more details about her sister and why her sister is "fit for life."

Imagine that you wrote the same answer as Mia. Use the following questions to help you revise and improve your answer.

1. Have I stated my main idea clearly? If not, what do I need to add to my opening sentence?

   Write the revised sentence here.

   _____

   _____

   _____

2. Have I explained how exercise makes my sister fit for life? If not, what details do I need to add?

   Expand Sentence 2 into a paragraph. Make sure you use details from the selection and from observing your sister. Write your new paragraph here.

   _____

   _____

   _____

   _____

   _____

   _____

   _____

   _____

3. Have I explained how running makes my sister fit for life? If not, what details do I need to add?

   Expand Sentence 3 into a paragraph. Make sure you use details from the selection and from observing your sister. Write your new paragraph here.

   _____

   _____

   _____

   _____

   _____

   _____

   _____

   _____

SCORE BUILDER

Many open-ended questions ask you to use details from the reading selection. Here is one way that Terrell used a detail from the selection in his answer:

The President's Council on Physical Fitness and Sports says you need to be able to do these two things.

Notice that Terrell used the name of the group mentioned in the selection—the President's Council on Physical Fitness and Sports.

Read the sentences below. Each sentences calls attention to information and details found in the selection. Circles the words that call attention to the information and details.

1. Our gym class meets five times a week, the way the article suggests.

2. The President's Council on Physical Fitness and Sports says that exercise can help keep you from getting sick.

3. The reading selection mentions that skating, biking, and yoga are good kinds of exercise.

4. According to the selection, we need to exercise hard for at least half an hour each day.

Lesson 21

Responding on Your Own

Here is another question about the selection *Fit for Life*. This time you will write your own answer. You won't have any models or questions to help you. As you plan and write your answer, think about what you have learned from studying Terrell's answer and improving Mia's answer. You should also use the following things to help you write your answer:

✓ **the strategy** you have practiced (making connections)

✓ the tips you were given in **Tools & Tips**

✓ the reminders in the **Score Builder**

> **Imagine that your school has decided to help students become fit for life. What kind of gym program do you think your school should have? How should your gym classes change? Use your own ideas and information from the reading selection in your answer.**

Notice that this question is like the first two. It asks you to connect your own experience to the information in the reading selection.

_____

_____

_____

_____

_____

_____

_____

_____

_____

_____

HINT!

Remember that the test scorers look for the following things:

✳ A clear statement of the main idea.

✳ Supporting details from both the reading selection and your own ideas.

✳ Clear and complete sentences.

✳ Don't forget to do the SLAMS test, too!

Reader's Response!
Revise & Edit

When you have finished writing, exchange papers with a partner. As you read each other's work, answer the questions below.

1 Did the writer answer the question?   ___Yes ___ No

2 Do the writer's ideas make sense?   ___ Yes ___ No
If you yes, explain why. If no, explain why not.
Write your response here.

_____

_____

_____

3 Did the writer give examples from his or her   ___ Yes ___ No
own experience?
If not, what needs to be added or changed?
Write your response here.

_____

_____

_____

4 Has the writer followed all the SLAMS rules?   ___ Yes ___ No
If not, which rules were not followed?
Check all the rules that apply.

S ___   L ___   A ___   M ___   S ___

5 **Give the paper back to your partner to revise and edit.**

Reviewing the Question

A question that asks you to read beyond the lines may be asked in different ways. Read the questions below. Pay attention to the words in **dark type**.

- **What have you learned** about making new friends from this story?

- Did John do the right thing? Support your answer with **your own ideas and experiences**, as well details from the selection.

- Think of a time when a friend disappointed you. **How did you feel? What did you do?**

- How would you convince a friend to try something new? Use **your own ideas and experiences** to support your answer.

- Use details from the selection and **your own observations** to explain why Carla was so unhappy.

- **Would you have made the same choice** as Carla? Why or why not?

Reviewing the Question

Watch out for words like the ones in dark type on page 106. Many open-ended questions may ask you to:

- connect the reading selection with something that you have experienced yourself;

- explain decisions or choices you would have made;

- compare your experiences with those of the characters;

- make predictions based on your own experiences.

To answer questions like these, you need to refer to ideas and experiences that are not in the reading selection.

Read the selection and answer the questions
that follow.

At the Top of the World

"I think I am the first man to sit on top of the world,"
said Matthew Henson. It was April 6, 1909. Henson, along
with Robert Peary, was on a trip to the North Pole. He was
the first man—and the first African American—to travel so
far north.

How did Matthew Henson get so far north? It was a
long journey. Henson was born in Maryland in 1886. By the
time he was eleven years old, he was an orphan. He didn't
have time for school because he was always working.
Matthew was almost thirteen years old, and he still didn't
know how to read.

Then he got a job on a ship. The captain of the ship liked
him. So, with the captain's help, Matthew was able to study as
well as work. The captain taught Matthew how to read, write,
and do math. Matthew also studied history and geography. He
learned how to read maps and how to sail a ship.

When he was eighteen, Matthew Henson returned to
dry land. He worked in a store in Washington, D.C. That's
where he met the explorer Robert Peary. Peary was getting
ready to go to Nicaragua in Central America. He asked
Henson to go along and help him. Matthew was eager to
travel to faraway places. He took the job.

The two men spent two years in Nicaragua, exploring
the jungle. They were looking for a way to build a canal.
Peary saw that Henson was a good mechanic. Henson was
also a carpenter and could build many things. Maybe most
important for an explorer, Henson was a navigator. He knew
how to find his way in the middle of nowhere, and he could
draw maps of where he had been.

Peary hired Henson to go to Greenland with him. This was their first trip to the Arctic. They explored Greenland to find out how far north the island went. As they explored, they also drew maps. They hoped to be able to travel all the way to the North Pole some day. It would take more than one trip to the Arctic to learn all they needed to know.

The many trips they made to the Arctic were very important for Henson and Peary. They learned the dangers of traveling on ice. The water under the ice can cause the ice to crack and break. Anyone on the ice can easily fall into the freezing water.

Henson tried to learn all he could from the native people, the Inuit. He learned how to build a dog sled and how to drive it. He learned how to build an igloo and how to hunt for meat in the frozen north. He also learned how to speak Inuktitut, the Inuit language. He was the only person in their group who could talk with the Inuit.

April 6, 1909, was their last attempt to reach the North Pole. Only six people were in their group. Henson, on foot, was in front. Behind him, Peary was on a sled being pulled by the Inuit. Peary said he had arrived at the North Pole first. He took all the credit for getting to the top of the world. Peary got all the awards from groups like the National Geographic Society and the United States Congress.

Without Matthew Henson, Peary might never have survived his trips to the Arctic. Henson had to wait until 1937 to be made a member of the Explorers Club, and he had to wait even longer to win a medal from Congress or from the president. It's only now that the world knows how important Matthew Henson was.

1 Reading What Is on the Page

The selection mentions several trips that Matthew Henson and Robert Peary took together. What were these trips? What was the purpose of each trip?

_____

_____

_____

_____

_____

_____

_____

_____

_____

_____

_____

_____

_____

_____

_____

_____

_____

_____

_____

_____

2 Reading Between the Lines

Matthew Henson and Robert Peary worked together for many years. How would you describe the relationship between them? Use your own ideas and details from the selection in your answer.

_____

_____

_____

_____

_____

_____

_____

_____

_____

_____

_____

_____

_____

_____

_____

_____

_____

_____

_____

_____

3 Reading Beyond the Lines

What do you think made Matthew Henson unusual? Use your own ideas and details from the selection to support your answer.

_____

_____

_____

_____

_____

_____

_____

_____

_____

_____

_____

_____

_____

_____

_____

_____

_____

_____

_____